CREEPY CRAWLIES

Slugs

by
Megan Borgert-Spaniol

BLASTOFF! READERS

BELLWETHER MEDIA · MINNEAPOLIS, MN

Note to Librarians, Teachers, and Parents:

Blastoff! Readers are carefully developed by literacy experts and combine standards-based content with developmentally appropriate text.

Level 1 provides the most support through repetition of high-frequency words, light text, predictable sentence patterns, and strong visual support.

Level 2 offers early readers a bit more challenge through varied simple sentences, increased text load, and less repetition of high-frequency words.

Level 3 advances early-fluent readers toward fluency through increased text and concept load, less reliance on visuals, longer sentences, and more literary language.

Level 4 builds reading stamina by providing more text per page, increased use of punctuation, greater variation in sentence patterns, and increasingly challenging vocabulary.

Level 5 encourages children to move from "learning to read" to "reading to learn" by providing even more text, varied writing styles, and less familiar topics.

Whichever book is right for your reader, Blastoff! Readers are the perfect books to build confidence and encourage a love of reading that will last a lifetime!

This edition first published in 2016 by Bellwether Media, Inc.

No part of this publication may be reproduced in whole or in part without written permission of the publisher. For information regarding permission, write to Bellwether Media, Inc., Attention: Permissions Department, 5357 Penn Avenue South, Minneapolis, MN 55419.

Library of Congress Cataloging-in-Publication Data

Borgert-Spaniol, Megan, 1989- author.
  Slugs / by Megan Borgert-Spaniol.
    pages cm. – (Blastoff! readers. Creepy Crawlies)
  Summary: "Developed by literacy experts for students in kindergarten through grade three, this book introduces slugs to young readers through leveled text and related photos"–Provided by publisher.
  Audience: Ages 5-8.
  Audience: K to grade 3.
  Includes bibliographical references and index.
  ISBN 978-1-62617-301-9 (hardcover : alk. paper)
  1. Slugs (Mollusks)–Juvenile literature. I. Title. II. Series: Blastoff! readers. 1, Creepy crawlies.
  QL430.4.B67 2016
  594.3–dc23
                                        2015029856

Table of Contents

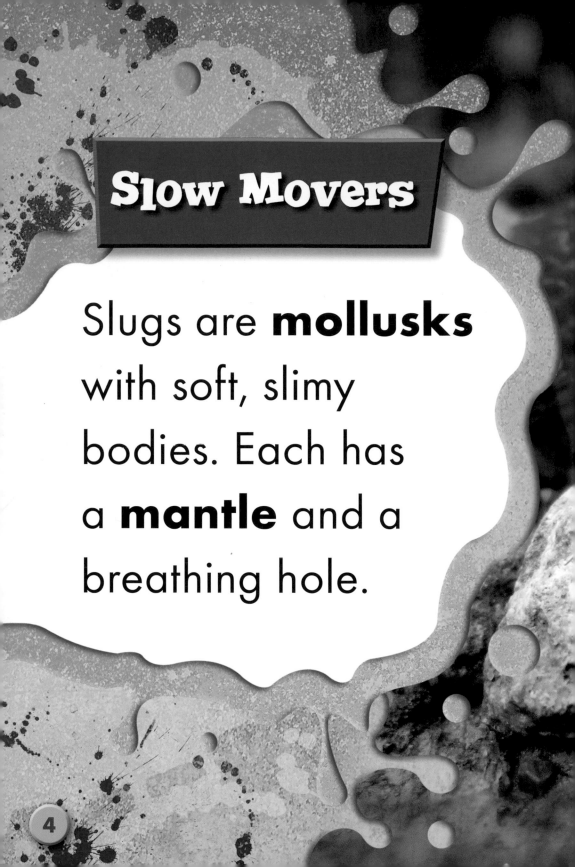

Slow Movers

Slugs are **mollusks** with soft, slimy bodies. Each has a **mantle** and a breathing hole.

breathing
hole

mantle

Slugs live in forests, fields, and gardens. They move slowly on a **foot**.

foot

They use **tentacles** to see and smell.

Day and Night

Slugs can dry up in the sun. They stay **underground** or in the shade during the day.

They come
out at night or
when it rains.

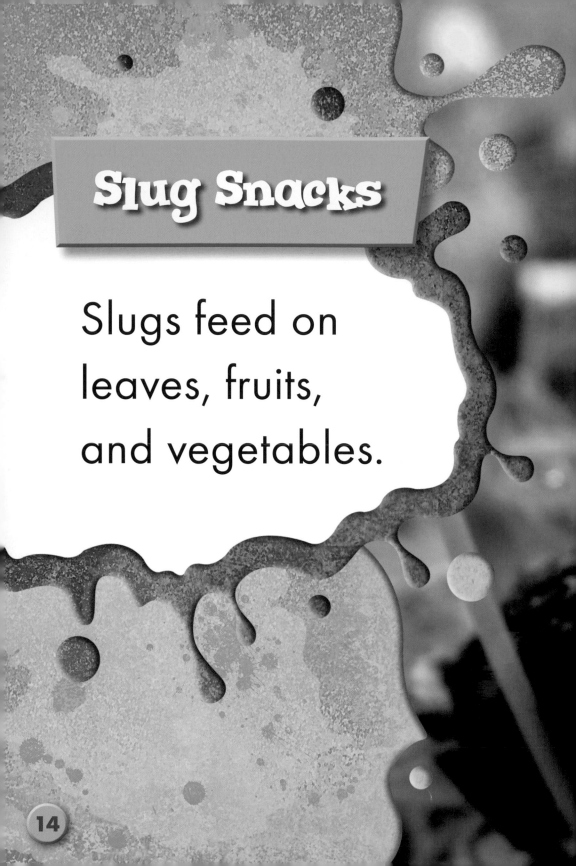

Slug Snacks

Slugs feed on leaves, fruits, and vegetables.

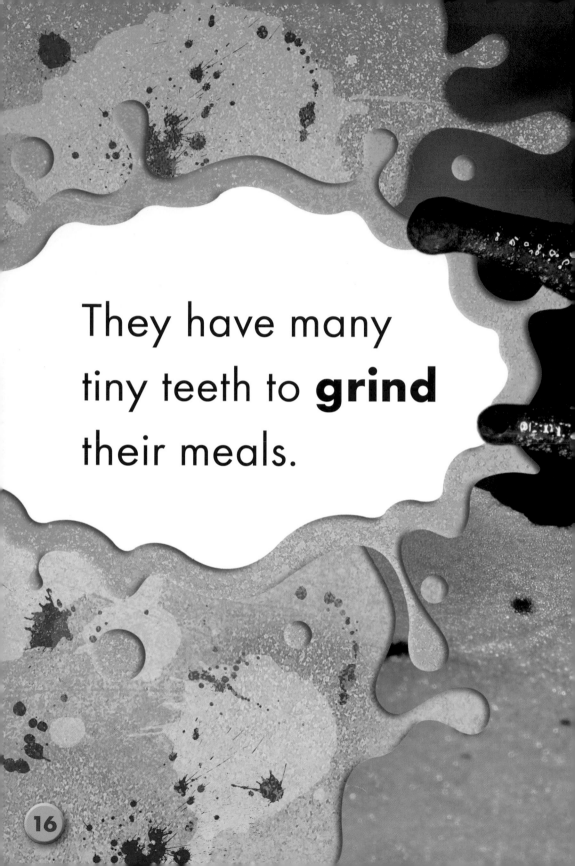

They have many tiny teeth to **grind** their meals.

Slime

Slugs are covered in slime. It helps keep them wet.

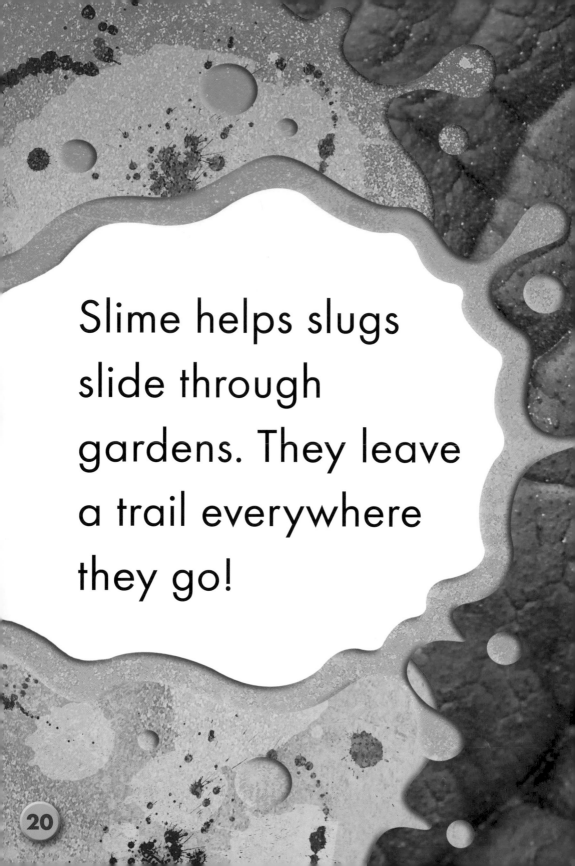

Slime helps slugs slide through gardens. They leave a trail everywhere they go!

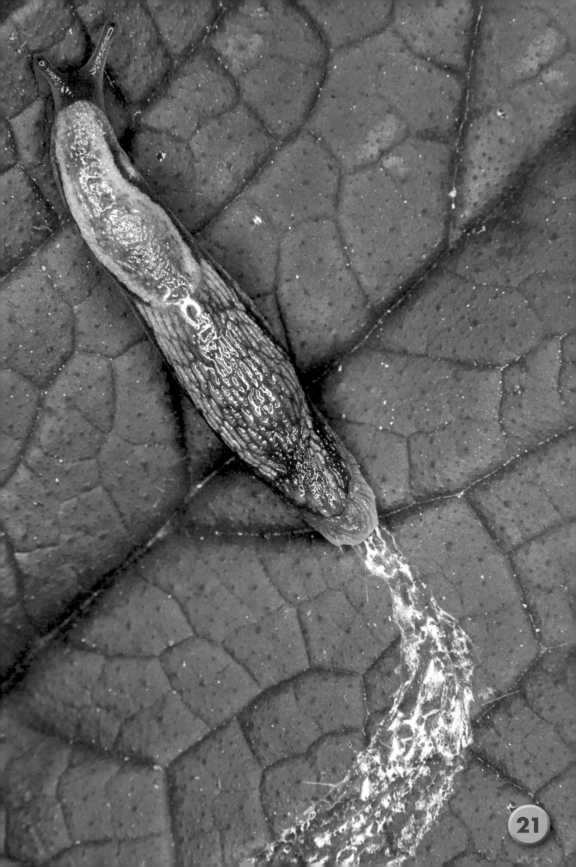

Glossary

foot—a flat muscle on the bottom side of a slug; the foot makes slime and moves a slug forward.

grind—to crush into smaller bits

mantle—a fold of thick skin that keeps a slug's body safe

mollusks—animals that have soft bodies and no backbones; slugs, clams, and octopuses are types of mollusks.

tentacles—soft, bendable parts that stick out from the heads of some animals; slugs have two sets of tentacles.

underground—below the ground

To Learn More

AT THE LIBRARY

Bishop, Celeste. *Slimy Slugs*. New York, N.Y.: PowerKids Press, 2016.

Bodden, Valerie. *Slugs*. Mankato, Minn.: Creative Paperbacks, 2014.

Willis, Jeanne. *Slug Needs a Hug!* Minneapolis, Minn.: Andersen Press Picture Books, 2015.

ON THE WEB

Learning more about slugs is as easy as 1, 2, 3.

1. Go to www.factsurfer.com.

2. Enter "slugs" into the search box.

3. Click the "Surf" button and you will see a list of related web sites.

With factsurfer.com, finding more information is just a click away.

Index